Julie Snow Architects

Foreword by Thomas Fisher
Essay by Janet Abrams

Princeton Architectural Press New York

Graham Foundation | Princeton Architectural Press
New Voices in Architecture
presents first monographs on emerging designers
from around the world

Also available in this series:

Rick Joy: Desert Works
1-56898-366-0

ARO: Architecture Research Office
Stephen Cassell and Adam Yarinsky
1-56898-367-0

An Architecture of the Ozarks: The Works of Marlon Blackwell
1-56898-488-X

Published by
Princeton Architectural Press
37 East Seventh Street
New York, New York 10003

For a free catalog of books, call 1.800.722.6657.
Visit our web site at www.papress.com.

Publication of this book has been supported by a grant from
the Graham Foundation for Advanced Studies in the Fine Arts.

Editing: Linda Lee and Mark Lamster
Design: Andrew Blauvelt
Design Assistance: Kyle Blue, Silas Munro, David Naj,
Daniel Winden

Jacket photography: Brian Vanden Brink
Cover photography: Tim Hursley

Special thanks to: Nettie Aljian, Nicola Bednarek, Janet
Behning, Megan Carey, Penny (Yuen Pik) Chu, Russell
Fernandez, Jan Haux, Clare Jacobson, John King, Nancy
Eklund Later, John McGill, Katharine Myers, Jane Sheinman,
Scott Tennent, Jennifer Thompson, Joseph Weston, and
Deb Wood of Princeton Architectural Press
—Kevin C. Lippert, publisher

Library of Congress Cataloging-in-Publication Data

Julie Snow Architects/foreword by Thomas Fisher;
essay by Janet Abrams.
    p. cm.—(New voices in architecture)
  Includes bibliographical references.
  ISBN 1-56898-487-1 (pbk.: alk. paper)
1. Julie Snow Architects. 2. Snow, Julie. 3. Architec-
ture—United States—20th century. 4. Architecture—United
States—21st century. I. Snow, Julie. II. Abrams, Janet.
III. Julie Snow Architects. IV. Series.

NA737.J85A4 2005
720'.092'2—dc22
                                         2004015063

Julie Snow Architects

Foreword: Heir Apparent
Thomas Fisher

Julie Snow is heir to the Case Study House program. Begun sixty years ago by John Entenza of *Arts & Architecture* magazine, the thirty-six Case Study houses, mostly built in Southern California, represented a high point in modern American architecture. They combined the social ideal of improving the lives of ordinary people through good design with the technological ideal of harnessing industrial science to minimize the materiality of buildings. Both values were largely lost in the architectural excesses and extremes of recent decades, which makes their reappearance in the work of Julie Snow even more extraordinary.

While Snow has designed relatively few houses, the ethics and aesthetics of the Case Study House program pervade her work. Her design for the Origen Center—with its long, low forms, minimal steel framing, panelized exterior walls, and thinly mullioned glass walls connecting the interior to outdoor terraces—recalls the lightness and openness of Craig Ellwood's 1955 Case Study House #17. Likewise, her polycarbonate office enclosure for Product Engineering brings to mind Ellwood's use of translucent-glass screen walls in Case Study Houses #16 and #18, from 1953 and 1958, respectively. Snow's Koehler House, with its glass pavilion cantilevered over its sloping site, echoes Pierre Koenig's 1960 Case Study House #22, while her QMR and Short Run Production plants, whose single volumes contain offices and production areas separated by glass walls, evoke the connection between the glass-walled house and the high-bay atrium in Edward Killingsworth's 1962 Case Study houses #25 and #26. Finally, her Jerstad Center, with its mix of housing, offices, and social space arranged around an outdoor terrace and pool, reminds us of the last Case Study project, Killingsworth's elegantly minimal 1964 design for live/work apartments clustered around a common terrace and pool.

Those formal connections express an underlying environmental idea. The Case Study House program, initiated in an era of material shortages during World War II, showed how we might build using fewer resources—a lesson also relevant to our own time of diminishing fossil fuels and disappearing rain forests. Snow's work suggests that making buildings more environmentally sustainable may depend as much upon using fewer yet more durable materials as it does upon using "green" ones.

If Snow's architecture goes against the conventional wisdom of sustainability, so too does her practice, which defies easy classification. Relatively few architects have her mix of projects: rail stations, bridges, pet collars, telematic tables. In such odd juxtapositions, Snow's projects recall those of Charles and Ray Eames. Their 1949 Case Study House #8—the most influential of all the houses built during the program—became their home and studio in which they produced a remarkable range of designed products, such as films, furniture, tapestries, and toys. The Eameses refused to abide by the specialization that had overtaken design since World War II, and so has Julie Snow. Compared to the Eames' body of work, Snow's SecurePet ID Collar has a similar sense of humor; her Telematic Table for the Walker Art Center possesses a related multimedia sophistication; and her Midtown Greenway Bridges' light- and soundscapes share a comparable sensory appeal.

Snow has a direct connection to the Case Study program via Ralph Rapson, one of the last of the Case Study architects still living and working: Snow has taught in, lectured at, and juried for the architecture program at the University of Minnesota, which Rapson headed for thirty years. Indeed, these two architects—both Michigan natives whose careers have flourished in Minnesota's snow country—remain mutual admirers of each other's work. Rapson himself has carried on the Case Study tradition. His unbuilt 1945 Case Study House #4, the Greenbelt House, inspired his recent entry into a low-cost housing competition sponsored by *Dwell* magazine, a design that Wieler Homes in North Carolina has put into production. Meanwhile, Snow's design for a software developer's headquarters, with a site plan consisting of long bar buildings pulled apart to capture outdoor space, looks like a Greenbelt House all grown up and gone off to work.

Such visual similarities reveal an underlying ethical idea. The critic Esther McCoy wrote that "the Case Study houses were an idealized mirror of an age in which an emerging pragmatism veiled Rooseveltian idealism." Those houses, in other words, represented a very different ethical stance toward modernism than the ideologically driven work of European architects or the corporately beholden work of many American architects of that era. Combining the social idealism of the one with the economic realism of the other, the Case Study architects pursued a pragmatic interest in programmatic and technical experimentation within the limits of what average families could afford. A similar pragmatism informs Snow's work. In a recent submission to an urban design competition in Winnipeg, Manitoba, Snow's office proposed a series of experiments called Urban Seeding, which mixed activities such as jogging, socializing, and people watching with standard urban infrastructure like benches, bus stops, and bollards to see what interactions might result.

That practical ethic of experimentation and evaluation, of testing ideas and reflecting on their meaning, has great consequences that are often overlooked. In our own age of resource scarcity and social inequity, neither utopian fantasies nor cynical critiques will get us anywhere. Instead, it will take the quiet boldness and radical humility that characterized the Case Study houses and that continues to this day in the far-reaching work of Julie Snow.

Thomas Fisher is dean of the College of Architecture and Landscape Architecture at the University of Minnesota and former editorial director of *Progressive Architecture* magazine. He has most recently written a book on the work of architect David Salmela; an introduction to a book on twelve houses by Bohlin, Cywinski, Jackson; and a preface to a book on the architecture of Fox & Fowle.

Craig Ellwood, Fields House, Case Study House #18, 1956–58. Courtesy Archives–Special Collections, College of Environmental Design, California State Polytechnic University, Pomona, CA

Julie Snow Architects, Origen Center, 1994. Photo: Don Wong

The work of a studio is in some ways framed by its earliest projects. Our first clients were manufacturing engineers; our first projects were industrial facilities. The projects were functional and pragmatic yet criti-cal of the conventional workplace, establishing an alternative version of industrial production spaces. The designs blurred the division between management and production and, with daylight, transformed the daily work experience. The architecture offered little that was unnecessary or indulgent. The directed, purposeful set of values that evolved within these projects was reiterated and expanded upon in future pro-posals. Ideas within the studio are tested by our design version of Occam's razor, which suggests that the most direct and obvious strategy may also be the most compelling.

Our work does not begin with a preconceived agenda that is applied to all projects but, rather, responds to the conditions presented by each scenario. The authenticity of architecture, for us, is found not in the demonstration of theoretical positions brought to it, but in how it reveals the actual conditions and situations that create the need for architecture. Our conceptual groundwork is found within the project's unique programmatic, contextual, and constructional circumstances. Programmatic requirements include not only the functional needs of the building but also the broadest—possibly the most profound—implications of its activities. Defining the building's performance by its ability to comfortably support both the specific activities of the program, as well as more broadly constructed goals, challenges programmatic conventions. The specifics of each project contribute to a redefinition of normative models. These innovations are not artificially imposed, but result from an investigation of the specifics of each program.

Likewise, the site is considered for opportunities, limitations, and possible contradictions. The physicality and experience of the context is explored as the conceptual foundation for the architecture. The mutual interaction between architecture and context intensifies each as an experience. Site constraints create additional requirements for architectural performance. Contradictions or tensions imbedded in the project context are revealed and amplified, rather than resolved. For example, the police department's requirement for security and the Fifth Precinct neighborhood's demand for openness create tension in the architecture. Similarly, the fragility of the New Brunswick landscape that requires light construction conflicts with the threatening climate that demands a grounded sense of enclosure.

When inserting a new activity into a site, architecture becomes a point of friction, acting as the mediator between purpose and place. The design process extracts qualities of site and activity, creates a dialogue between the two, and transforms each. Architecture reveals and intensifies that transformation.

Given a frugality of formal expression, the wall—its assembly, materials, and detailing—often acts as the mediator between place and activity, which in turn fuels our constructional investigation. For example, most of our structures operate in extremely harsh environments that require a hardier wall; we counter expectations by creating enclosures that are thinner, lighter, and stronger. Robustness is achieved through a rigorous assembly requiring precise construction. At certain moments within the design process, the work may verge on the banal; creating constructional systems that begin with conventional assemblies yet offer a higher level of performance elevates the work from the ordinary. The aim is not to confound expectations, but to raise them.

Our methodology begins with a deferral of design in favor of research into the proposed project. We intentionally quiet our voice, allowing the project to formulate itself; there is no critical agenda within the process. As the project develops its own specific design agenda, it creates its own differentiation. Our search is focused on finding, within the myriad conditions of the project, its challenge—a contradiction, perhaps, or apparent mutually exclusive requirements. Architecture is not proposed as a resolution but as an articulation of these oppositions. Moving from research to design, we begin to develop strategies addressing building systems from a technical position. Starting with a critique of conventional systems, we explore ways to modify or enhance their performance. We engage in intensive questioning, reasserting and testing different approaches against the performance criteria as the design evolves.

The defining characteristic of a collaborative studio environment is the shared conceptual development of the projects. Our designers consistently test and challenge generative concepts as the architectural exploration fragments into parallel investigations of building components. This environment requires an articulation of the underlying investigation of the studio as a whole as well as the inquiries specific to each project.

Our studio has intentionally avoided a specialist role in project types. The diversity of our work requires that we research each project and remain open to its unique demands. As we engage in more complex projects, we develop collaborative design teams with specialists. These collaborations have extended beyond the studio and into projects that are outside traditional boundaries of architecture. They are not an adjunct to the work effort but are essential to the conceptualization and realization of a project. Exposure to other design disciplines and to issues that challenge our assumptions about the limits of architecture's domain have made a vital contribution to the energy of the studio.

If directness and pragmatism drove the earlier work, more recent projects expand on this approach. Rather than seeking transformative moments within a client's functional agenda, we address our client's transformative agenda with pragmatic strategies. For instance, in the Midtown Greenway Bridges, the community sought to attract pedestrians to a little-used transitway. A light and sound environment below the bridges enables a sense of play and offers another dimension to an otherwise (literally) pedestrian experience. A recently completed design competition proposal sought to enliven a metropolitan intersection by adding unexpected functional components to typical urban infrastructural elements, thereby increasing the possibilities of how we use our cities. Recent projects explore architecture's magnetic quality, its ability to attract and to engage. On the University of South Dakota Business School proposal, the shimmering quality of the skin mesmerizes the viewer and blurs the apparent boundary of the building.

The trajectory of the studio's work depends on our clients' proposals. We have been fortunate to work with many clients that challenge us as we challenge them. We are grateful for their confidence. Over the past years, I have been honored to work with an extraordinarily talented, committed group of architects. Our engineering and construction colleagues have been consistently bold, resourceful, and creative. Their investment in our collaborations is greatly appreciated. In this opportunity to share our work with others, I am grateful to Kevin Lippert, Mark Lamster, and Linda Lee at Princeton Architectural Press for their patience and their prodding. Thanks also to Tom Fisher and Jan Abrams for their reflections and consideration of the work. I am deeply indebted to Andrew Blauvelt not only for his book design, but also for our many conversations enlivened by his insight into art, design, and architecture. Last but never least, I am grateful to my family, Jack, Anne, Kate, and David, for bearing with me when my profession frequently turned to obsession. Finally, I must thank my parents, Dr. and Mrs. A. R. VandenBerg for their faith and support.

Julie Snow: The Rugged and the Refined
Janet Abrams

A luminous white aerie on the twenty-fourth floor of the Rand Tower in downtown Minneapolis, commanding a rare, Manhattan-worthy view of the surrounding skyscrapers: the HQ of Julie Snow Architects. The red dot matrix of the TCF building's clock pierces the nighttime panorama. In the far left corner sits the principal of the firm, at work on her G4 laptop—all the toys are black, white, or silver. She's talking on the phone, but periodically, instead of finishing a sentence, she'll throw back her head and emit a voluptuous chuckle—a vocal signature that elides language and laughter, erupting frequently in conversation.

You might not guess this aspect of Snow's personality from her buildings, which tend to be on the abstemious side, not playing for laughs. But the chortle gives it away—underneath it all, she's a playful person. It's just that the game is serious, and Snow has a taste for the tough stuff—engineering, construction, the rigors and logic of building assembly—and architecture is, even in this first decade of the twenty-first century, still considered (effectively) a man's world.

Luxury in Austerity
Snow's buildings are spartan—at least, they may strike one as such at first glance—but also luxurious in their austerity, in a way that recalls seventeenth-century Dutch still-life paintings with their contradictory surface expressions of frugality and abundance. Her concern seems to be with creating a taut, precise framework for the enactment of daily life rituals, enabling them but not overdetermining them by imposing a heavily stylized environment in which the user feels obliged to conform to the behavioral dictates of the architect. There is a reticence to her architecture that some may find too astringent, wishing for a more explicit voice or more forceful personality. Snow resists, in favor of establishing finely detailed environments wrought out of structural and social necessities and a relish for the crafts of building engineering and assembly: a glass wall that appears to hang free of its support structure in the Great Plains Software project; a turnbuckle that pulls together the weight of a roof in an inner-city police station; the tracery of stellar con-

stellations on a transit stop's glass canopy. Her aesthetic—wresting elegance out of prefabricated parts and industrial assembly systems—has developed through close collaboration with contractors, building component manufacturers, and most particularly with engineers: Arup, the international engineering firm, is a regular collaborator. "I'm not an engineer," she volunteers. "But I'm really good at *talking* to engineers, listening to them." (She's also married to one: Jack Snow.)

Life in the Vast Lane
Spot the black speck making steady progress across a vast, flat, arable landscape. Zero in and the speck turns out to be a BMW 530i driven at high speed across the Great Plains. In the driver's seat is a woman dressed in monochrome, focused on the far horizon, Philip Glass at full blast on the stereo. Destination: maybe Fargo, North Dakota, or perhaps this time it's Sioux Falls, South Dakota. Who can tell these states apart? The plains are the plains after all. A police car appears in pursuit, pulls up beside the car, which, even in the midst of a grit-strewn midwestern winter, is immaculately shiny. The driver's window rolls down; she lowers her tortoiseshell glasses and pleads, "Officer, I had *no idea* I was going that fast." With a caution, he lets the Emma Peel of architecture go.

Fargo is an unlikely spot on Earth for a cutting-edge software development company. But the freedom and openness of the landscape inspires the corporate ethos of Great Plains Software, and hence its desire for an uninterrupted creative environment for its growing workforce—expanded from 10 people to 650 in fifteen years. Two long bars are mutually offset to maximize views, especially through the south bar's glass facade, and interspersed by equivalent slabs of landscaping, emulating the "shelterbelts" that protect crops from the climatic savagery of the open plains.

People think of the plains as unarticulated bland space, but to me it's extremely profound. There isn't a topographically determined path across it, so you have to make a decision about where you want to be.

This is a particularly American quality: a vast, un-restricted democratic country in which everyone has opportunity. There was no program, no org. chart, for the Great Plains Software project. They simply said, "We want the building in eighteen months. GO!"

So Snow gathered the clients and engineers in her office for a three-day charette to design the building systems and the ubiquitous IT, developing program and landscape in tandem. Together they devised the most efficient way to span forty-eight feet without interruption—rolled I-sections bolted to round columns. The undivided floor space echoes the seemingly limit-less terrain of the Dakota Plains while meeting the soft-ware developer's needs for spatial flexibility and fast telecommunications throughout, accommodating their fluctuating cycles of individual and group activity.

> The buildings create a dialog with the landscape. This huge plain of space allows the users to reconfigure their work environment and navigate it in as free a way as possible. It's like the deck of a battleship, but the tools are there to connect the team members to the broadest bandwidth.

Breathing More Slowly
Transparency, clarity of vision, landscape, and light—these are the principal subjects of Snow's architecture, though not always explicitly so. Her buildings are often taken to be exercises in minimalism. Lest that seems simply reductive, here's the real aim: the stripping back of architectural "noise" to achieve a state of quietness in which a building's occupants can perceive the quality of the landscape in which their building is set, notice the quotidian passage of light through all the shades of daytime, into dusk, evening, night. Asked when she herself experiences these moments of repose, Snow re-sponds, "When I'm taking the dog for a walk in the morning, around the lake."

Introspection. Reflection. Meditation. These are the states of calm that her buildings induce and which her clients seek her out to create. She talks of her aspiration toward creating "transformative" architectural experi-

ences, those that still the mind. Spaces that invite you to "just start breathing a little more slowly."

> I look at architecture as a playing field on which people operate. It's all about making connections between places and activities, site and architecture. Our work is not reductive. It's *inclusive*—but not overly complete or complex, so it has room for other things. In a really beautiful room, an unmade bed looks good.

Bowls of Light
There are characteristic tropes: the insistent rectilinear forms and horizontal massing; low-rise buildings that seem to hug the ground, grow long and thin out of their locations, their proportions and facades reminiscent of Dutch modernism; buildings as vessels for the harvesting of light.

Snow grew up in Michigan, as Julie VandenBerg, in a Dutch Reform household whose spiritual strictures and disdain for frippery or material flamboyance seems to have had an enduring impact on her aesthetic sensi-bilities. John Dinkeloo, founding partner in the archi-tecture firm Roche Dinkeloo, was a high-school friend of her father's. Yet it was her mother who, impressed by the diversity of Dinkeloo's activities and travel oppor-tunities, encouraged her daughter to take up architec-ture. Snow began her studies at the University of Colorado at Boulder, where she experienced a different kind of luminosity.

> In Colorado the light is intense. The light in Michigan is like the plains: it's very uniform and has almost a spatial quality. You're in a *bowl* of light—it's diffuse rather than coming from a source. It's spatial rather than directional.

Leaf through this monograph and you will see buildings that glow, especially at night—twinkling despite their conspicuous lack of architectural rhinestones. The Minneapolis Light Rail Transit Stations should perhaps be called the Rail Light Transit Stations since Snow uses light and structure to create urban beacons, using an elemental structural grid—riblike bays that delineate rather than enclose space—to confer brief instances of aesthetic coherence on the new transit system. (Ultimately, unity is defeated by the transit authority's determination to commission "context-specific" designs for the different stops, from a range of architect/artist teams.)

Of the three stations Snow was commissioned to design, two were realized in collaboration with artist Tom Rose, and the third was lost to the scrum of metropolitan design politics. At the Cedar-Riverside station, in a modest neighborhood that has become home to many of Minneapolis' East-African immigrants, the station canopy is glass and decorated with the celestial constellations that might be seen through it. At the Lake Street stop, astride a junction beset with big-box retailers, franchise foods, and parking lots, and possessed of limited urban charm, the station is like a candelabra for a less-than-glamorous part of the city. On this filigree bridge, linear bands of pastel-colored light cling to its illuminated ribs, high and beckoning, offering an ethereal palette against the night—a taste of Mies-meets-Flavin on a $1.75 transit ride.

Perhaps it has something to do with the CAD-rendering software Snow's firm uses that her buildings often seem to bask in an impossibly sharp and delineating sunlight—the kind that gives each figure in the scene an intensely etched outline, as if we too must be as firm and precise around our edges as her buildings aspire to be. Perhaps this is too much to ask of mere mortals. Take the University of South Dakota Business School, for example. A competition entry (alas, not to be realized), this building would have had an extraordinary shimmering facade. A set of clear, rectangular volumes pierce the ground-hugging main structure, cleaves its semiopaque surface—all the better to emphasize the gorgeousness of its surface, crystalline and seductive in its variegated translucencies. There's a comment here about the deceptive allure of the shiny—albeit not metal but glass—perhaps befitting an academic department dedicated to the dissemination of techniques for making and managing money.

Points of Abrasion

Snow speaks of always trying to find a place within the conditions of a project or its site that suggests "a contradiction that architecture has to resolve"—the programmatic grit in the oyster, so to speak—"not really to resolve it, but to articulate it, by detailing it intensely." Often, this point of abrasion has to do with apparently irreconcilable needs: for shelter *and* exposure, for visual accessibility *and* physical security, for the pleasure of effulgent light *and* the comfort of penumbra.

In the Fifth Precinct police station in Minneapolis' Lyndale neighborhood, for example, the task was to make a building that would convey openness and congeniality to the surrounding community while maintaining a sense of security, and without turning it into a fortress. Here the solution was in "districting" the two main components by creating a large transparent community room at one end and a wing of brick-faced offices for the police officers at the other. Their windows and, thus, everyday work are visible from the street but protected by a low brick wall enclosing a lightwell.

In the Koehler House, on the dramatic coastline of New Brunswick, the challenge was to reconcile the simultaneously threatening and fragile aspects of the environment. Here, on the savage coast of the Bay of Fundy, the choreography of physical experience—alternating rhythms of tight and open spaces—accentuates the drama of the remarkable site.

It was so loud in the wind we could hardly talk. But as soon as you walk down off the high point of the site, it becomes quiet and warm, and the landscape just holds you. You want both of those experiences in the house. As you come up the staircase, slotted between twelve-foot-high walls, you're very contained. Then suddenly you're connected physically and visually to the bold ocean view. It's a trajectory, this idea of projecting yourself into the landscape. You want to be both protected and connected, to huddle next to the fireplace, or to stand up on the top deck and exult.

Snow expresses a preference for sensual and spatial juxtapositions, which she tends to articulate in evocative catch phrases. "The thick/thin thing": pairing of solid and light structures. "The cave and the agora": sharp contrasts of dark, contained spaces with open, luminous expanses. "The rugged and the refined": natural textures and materials paired with high-tech industrial components—architecture as protection from harsh conditions, whether social or environmental.

Industrial Economies

Snow began designing factories at $90 per square foot. She has cut her teeth on utilitarian structures out in the middle of nowhere, industrial plants for the post-industrial economy—the Short Run Production facility in New Richmond, Wisconsin (a fast-order manufacturer of small, highly engineered parts); the Origen Center in Menomonie, Wisconsin (a business incubator cum corporate training facility); QMR in River Falls, Wisconsin (a fabricator of molded plastic parts). These buildings gain dignity from their relation of inside to outside; the emphasis on flooding the interiors with light so as to humanize them; by linking the prosaic, repetitive activities that go on within them to the ever-changing moods of the natural landscape without.

> We started out with very pragmatic building types, and we made a strategic choice between exploring more extravagant forms, or exploring details and assembly. You can't do both; you cannot do something interesting with the skin and the structure and *still* have a great deal of formal manipulation. We're a little "techie" at heart. I just really love construction—the way buildings are made—taking the assembly and refining it. I've always said: When I master Ninety Degrees, I'll move on.

Now she is on the cusp of change, from work that has been predominantly concerned with accommodating pragmatic functions toward an architecture that is "magnetic." From the days of ultra-minimalism, working on tight budgets to create new industrial spaces, she's progressed to making luxury homes out of former industrial structures along the Minneapolis riverfront. Her latest completed project combines conversion and new

construction, turning the former Gold Medal milling complex along the Mississippi River into loft condominiums for the city's wealthiest denizens and adding a brand new nine-story building that holds its own between the renovated historic facades of the Mill District (including the neighboring Mill City Museum) and the new Jean Nouvel-designed Guthrie Theater.

The oddities in the portfolio, the SecurePet ID Collar and the Telematic Table proposal for the Walker Art Center, signal Snow's ambition to transcend the boundaries between architecture and other design fields, such as product design and interactive media. Working with experts in other fields, from veterinary science to computer software, her firm has begun to address archi-tecture at scales very different from that of buildings. Whatever the form or purpose, the work is always graced with precision, attention to detail, a sensitivity to the play of light and transparency, and a seductive shimmer.

Janet Abrams is the founding director of the Design Institute at the University of Minnesota. She is the editor of *If/Then: Play*, published in 1998, and co-editor of *Else/Where: Mapping*, published by the Design Institute in 2004.

Chronology

1990
James/Snow Architects, Inc. formed.

Adjunct Professor, University of
Minnesota, College of Architecture
and Landscape Architecture,
Minneapolis, MN

Honor Award, AIA Minnesota, for Short
Run Production

1991–1997
Board of Directors, Secretary, Minnesota
Architectural Foundation

1994
Studio Syllabus Awards Jury, ACSA
Regional Conference

1995
Julie Snow Architects, Inc. formed.

Honor Award, AIA Minnesota,
for Phillips Plastics Corporation,
Origen Center

Honor Award, AIA Minnesota, for
Minnesota Children's Museum

1996
Honor Award, AIA Minnesota, for
QMR Production

1997
Architectural Record/Business Week
Award, for Origen Center

Bryant Memorial lecture on art and
architecture, Kansas State University,
College of Architecture, Planning, and
Design, Manhattan, KS

"Conditional Architecture" lecture,
University of Missouri, Department
of Architecture, Urban Planning, and
Design, Kansas City, MO

"Structure, Skin, Light Studies" lecture
and exhibition, Weisman Art Museum,
Minneapolis, MN

"Architecture's Performance" lecture,
ASLA/APA/AIA Joint Meeting, University
of Iowa, Ames, IA

1998
Architectural Record/Business Week
Award, for QMR Production

Honor Award, AIA Minnesota, for Fifth
Precinct Station

Honor Award, AIA Minnesota, for
Product Engineering

Brick Award, AIA Minnesota, for Fifth
Precinct Station

"Emerging Voices" lecture, the
Architectural League of New York, NY

Committee on Urban Environment
Award, for Fifth Precinct Station

AIA National Honor Award Jury,
Washington, DC

1999
Honor Award, AIA Minnesota, for
Jerstad Center, Good Samaritan Society

Design Distinction Award, *I.D.*
magazine, for Product Engineering

National Brick in Architecture Award,
Brick Industry Association, for
Fifth Precinct Station

Lecture, Chicago Architectural Club,
Chicago, IL

Lecture and exhibition, University of
Wisconsin, School of Architecture and
Urban Planning, Milwaukee, WI

Summer Design Series lecture,
Walker Art Center, AIA Minnesota,
Minneapolis, MN

Ralph Rapson Award for Distinguished
Teaching, University of Minnesota,
College of Architecture and Landscape
Architecture, Minneapolis, MN

Business Week/Architectural Record
Award Jury, Washington, DC

AIA Detroit Awards Jury

AIA Pittsburgh Honor Awards Jury

AIA St. Louis Honor Awards Jury

Girl Scouts of America Design Excellence Awards Jury

2000
Peer reviewer, Design Excellence
Program, U.S. General Services
Administration

"Assembly/Detail/Structure" lecture, AIA
Nebraska, Omaha, NE

"Case Studies" lecture, AIA Portland, OR

Lecture, AIA Memphis, TN

Elevated to the College of Fellows, American Institute of Architects

2001
Lecture, AIA Minnesota Annual Conference, Minneapolis, MN

"Design Energy" lecture, AIA Arkansas Annual Convention, Fayetteville, AR

"Conscience of Design: Commerce" lecture, AIA Ohio Valley, Annual Conference, Cincinnati, OH

Lecture, University of Florida, School of Architecture, Gainesville, FL

Lecture, Rice University, School of Architecture, Houston, TX

Bruce Goff Creative Chair lecture, University of Oklahoma, College of Architecture, Norman, OK

AIA Portland Awards Jury

AIA Nebraska Awards Jury

AIA Milwaukee Awards Jury

AIA Wisconsin Awards Jury

James Beard Foundation Design Awards Jury, New York, NY

2002
The Chicago Athenaeum: Museum of Architecture and Design, American Architecture Award, for Koehler House

Lecture, Yale University, School of Architecture, New Haven, CT

Lecture, San Francisco Museum of Modern Art, AIA San Francisco, CA

Lecture, University of Arkansas, School of Architecture, Fayetteville, AR

AIA Houston Awards Jury

2003
Honor Award, AIA Minnesota, for Koehler House

Spotlight on Design Series lecture, National Building Museum, Washington, DC

Lecture, North Carolina State University, College of Design, Raleigh, NC

Visiting Professor, University of Arkansas, School of Architecture, Fayetteville, AR

Lecture, University of Illinois, School of Architecture, Chicago, IL

Lecture, Washington University, School of Architecture, St. Louis, MO

Lecture, Philadelphia University, School of Architecture and Design, Philadelphia, PA

Lecture, Celebrate Architecture Conference, Baton Rouge, LA

Dupont Benedictus Glass Awards Jury, Washington, DC

2004
Minneapolis Heritage Preservation Commission Award, for Humboldt Mill

AIA St. Louis Awards Jury

AIA North Carolina Awards Jury

Selected Bibliography

2004
The Phaidon Atlas of Contemporary World Architecture. London and New York: Phaidon, 2004, 653. Koehler House.

2002
Jacobs, Peter, ed. *Abstract Magazine* 13 (May/June 2002): 26–31. Koehler House.

Jodidio, Philip. *Architecture Now!* Vol 2. Paris: Taschen Press, 2002. Koehler House.

Salangin, Alexander. "Flower in a Stone." *Komhatbi*, January 2002, 70–77. Koehler House.

2001
Bennecke, Sabine. "Wohndecks am Atlantik." *Bauwelt* 41/01, (November 2001): 24–27. Koehler House.

Fisher, Thomas. "Seaside Modernism." *Architecture Minnesota*, November/December 2001, 36–39. Koehler House.

Norman, Howard. "On Bold Ocean." *Dwell*, August 2001, 44–50. Koehler House.

Stephens, Suzanne. "Record Houses." *Architectural Record*, April 2001, 126–31. Koehler House.

1999
Cramer, Ned. "Plains Spoken." *Architecture*, October 1999, 100–05. Jerstad Center, Good Samaritan Society.

"I.D. Annual Design Review." *I.D. magazine*, July/August 1999, 175. Product Engineering.

LeFevre, Camille. "On The Prairie." *Architecture Minnesota*, November/December 1999, 30–33. Jerstad Center, The Good Samaritan Society.

1998
Crisp, Barbara. *Human Spaces, Life-Enhancing Designs for Healing Working and Living*. Gloucester, MA: Rockport Publishers, 1998, 70–75. QMR Production.

Keegan, Edward. "Street Patrol." *Architecture*, August 1998, 80–83. Fifth Precinct Station.

Kudalis, Eric. "Arresting Design." *Architecture Minnesota*, November/December 1998, 38–42. Fifth Precinct Station.

——— "Transparent Makeover." *Architecture Minnesota*, March/April 1999, 22–23. Product Engineering.

Nussbaum, Bruce. "Pride of Place; The Little Plant On The Prairie." *Business Week*, November 2, 1998, 62. QMR Production.

Pearman, Hugh. *Contemporary World Architecture*. London: Phaidon Press Limited, 1998, 316–17. Short Run Production, Origen Center, QMR Production.

Pearson, Clifford A. "A Factory for QMR Plastics Puts Workers and Managers under One Roof." *Architectural Record*, October 1998, 99. QMR Production.

1997
Carter, Brian. "Dignity of Labour." *The Architectural Review*, November 1997, 58–62. Origen Center, QMR Production.

Nussbaum, Harold. "Blue Prints for Business, Hotbed for Human Connections." *Business Week*, November 3, 1997, 132. Origen Center.

Russell, James. "Good Design is Good Business, Phillips Plastics Invents a New Building Type to Incubate Ideas." *Architectural Record*, October 1997, 57. Origen Center.

1996
Ghirado, Diane. *Architecture After Modernism*. London: Thames and Hudson, Ltd., 1996, 218–19. Short Run Production.

Kudalis, Eric. "Democratic Production." *Architecture Minnesota*, July/August 1996, 28–31. QMR Production.

——— "Manufacturing Ideas." *Architecture Minnesota*, January/February 1996, 24–27. Origen Center.

Landecker, Heidi. "Kid City." *Architecture*, November 1996, 86–93. Minnesota Children's Museum.

1995
Langdon, Phillip. "Factories for the Future." *Progressive Architecture*, November 1995, 49–57. Origen Center, QMR Production, Short Run Production.

Millet, Larry. "Play Land." *Architecture Minnesota*, November/ December 1995, 14–18. Minnesota Children's Museum.

Pearson, Clifford A. "Manufacturing Design in a Post Industrial Age." *Architectural Record*, August 1995, 86–87. Short Run Production, Origen Center.

1992
Pearson, Clifford A. "Industrial Resolution." *Architectural Record*, February 1992, 102–06. Short Run Production.

Studio Members

1995
Doug Coffler
Grant Reiling
Krista Scheib
Michael Sheridan
Craig Roberts
Cybele Hare
Mark Larson
Dan Clark

1996
Doug Coffler
Grant Reiling
Krista Scheib
Cybele Hare
Greg Larson
Mark Larson
Christian Dean
Ben Awes

1997
Doug Coffler
Grant Reiling
Krista Scheib
Cybele Hare
Greg Larson
Mark Larson
Christian Dean
Ben Awes
Robb Olsen

1998
Doug Coffler
Krista Scheib
Christian Dean
Ben Awes
Robb Olsen
Craig Roberts
Tom Van de Weghe
Todd Hemker

1999
Doug Coffler
Christian Dean
Ben Awes
Robb Olsen
Craig Roberts
Nina Broadhurst
Tom Van de Weghe
Tim Bicknell
Connie Lindor
Bob Ganser
Kenwood McQuade
Lucas Alm

2000
Christian Dean
Ben Awes
Robb Olsen
Craig Roberts
Nina Broadhurst
Tom Van de Weghe
Tim Bicknell
Connie Lindor
Bob Ganser
Kenwood McQuade
Lucas Alm
Chase DeForest
Tats Tanaka
Dan Clark
Erik Tietz

2001
Christian Dean
Ben Awes
Craig Roberts
Nina Broadhurst
Tom Van de Weghe
Tim Bicknell
Connie Lindor
Bob Ganser
Kenwood McQuade
Lucas Alm
Chase DeForest
Ernesto Ruiz García
Dan Vercruysse
Malini Srivastava
Martha McQuade
Takuma Handa
Alexis Burck

2002
Christian Dean
Ben Awes
Craig Roberts
Tim Bicknell
Bob Ganser
Lucas Alm
Chase DeForest
Ernesto Ruiz García
Dan Vercruysse
Malini Srivastava
Martha McQuade
Takuma Handa
John Cullen
Zoe Alder Resnick

2003
Christian Dean
Ben Awes
Craig Roberts
Tim Bicknell
Bob Ganser
Lucas Alm
Ernesto Ruiz García
Dan Vercruysse
Malini Srivastava
Martha McQuade
Takuma Handa
John Cullen
Matt Fajkus
Daniel Winden

Julie Snow Architects Selected Projects 1990–2004

Short Run Production New Richmond, Wisconsin 1990

The owner's intention to break from the conventional separation between management and production became the basis of this design. In another facility the client had installed four-by-eight-foot windows to connect office and production spaces. Expanding this idea, we proposed a single volume for the production and office spaces separated acoustically by steel-framed glass.

The site is located in an industrial park surrounded by a rolling rural landscape. Brick walls enclose the production floor to secure proprietary manufacturing processes. Above the brick, steel-bowstring trusses vault an eighty-foot workspace and filter daylight from above the trusses' spring line. The building's southeast corner is cut away to create an entry plaza, with the projecting trusses continuing the interior play of light and shadow to the exterior.

Project Team
(James/Snow Architects)
Julie Snow
Vincent James
Ali Heshmati
Chris Schmidt
Joe Statz
Jim Larson

Executive Architect: Mike Piene, PSI Design
Structural Engineer: Harwood Engineering
Mechanical Engineer: Irv Smith Engineering
Acoustic Consultant: Steve Kvernstoen
Contractor: Peter Schwabe Incorporated
Photographer: Don Wong
Owner: Phillips Plastics Corporation

upper-level plan

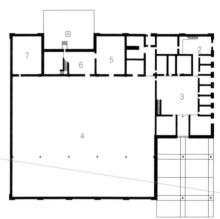

plan at grade

0 20 40 80

1. storage
2. lunchroom
3. offices
4. production space
5. toolroom
6. loading
7. raw-material storage

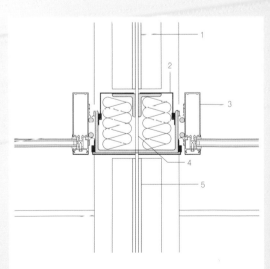

steel-truss wall-penetration plan detail
1. interior steel truss
2. break-metal enclosure
3. aluminum curtain wall
4. steel-knife plate connector
5. exterior steel truss

Origen Center Menomonie, Wisconsin 1994

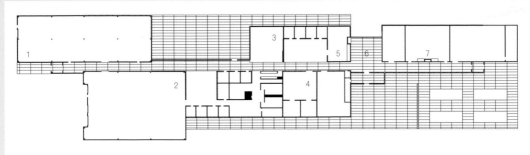

0   25   50

1. new business incubator
2. start-up manufacturing facility
3. lunchroom
4. training area
5. library
6. reception
7. meeting rooms

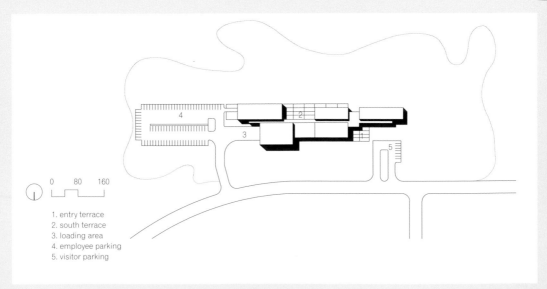

0   80   160

1. entry terrace
2. south terrace
3. loading area
4. employee parking
5. visitor parking

This project joined diverse functional elements, creating a hybrid programmatic type. A new business incubator, a start-up manufacturing facility, and a corporate-training function were all to have their own discrete focus within shared common areas. The goal was to facilitate the exchange of ideas and sharing of resources while maintaining the intensity and focus of the individual areas. The site was a level plane framed by geologic drumlins.

We began with an elongated structural steel grid standing on a granite plinth. Each program volume sits independently within this grid along a central spine. Taut enclosures of glass and cedar define distinct volumes of program. The resulting masses and voids respond to the grouping of the drumlins in the surrounding landscape. Steel-tube beams and deck are precisely detailed to be exposed throughout. Steel framing extends over exterior voids.

Project Team
(James/Snow Architects)
Julie Snow
Vincent James
Doug Coffler
Paul Gates
Paul Yaggie
Nancy Blankfard
Michael Sheridan
Nathan Knutson
Jim Larson
Krista Scheib

Structural Engineer: Meyer Borgman Johnson
Mechanical Engineer: Rand Systems
Electrical Engineer: B and B Electric
Landscape/Civil Engineer: Cedar Corporation
Contractor: Schwabe Construction
Photographer: Don Wong
Owner: Phillips Plastics Corporation

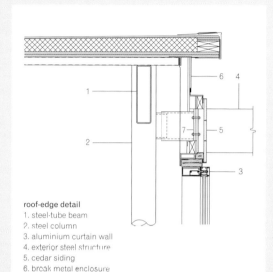

roof-edge detail
1. steel-tube beam
2. steel column
3. aluminium curtain wall
4. exterior steel structure
5. cedar siding
6. break metal enclosure
7. steel bolt connection

QMR Production River Falls, Wisconsin 1996

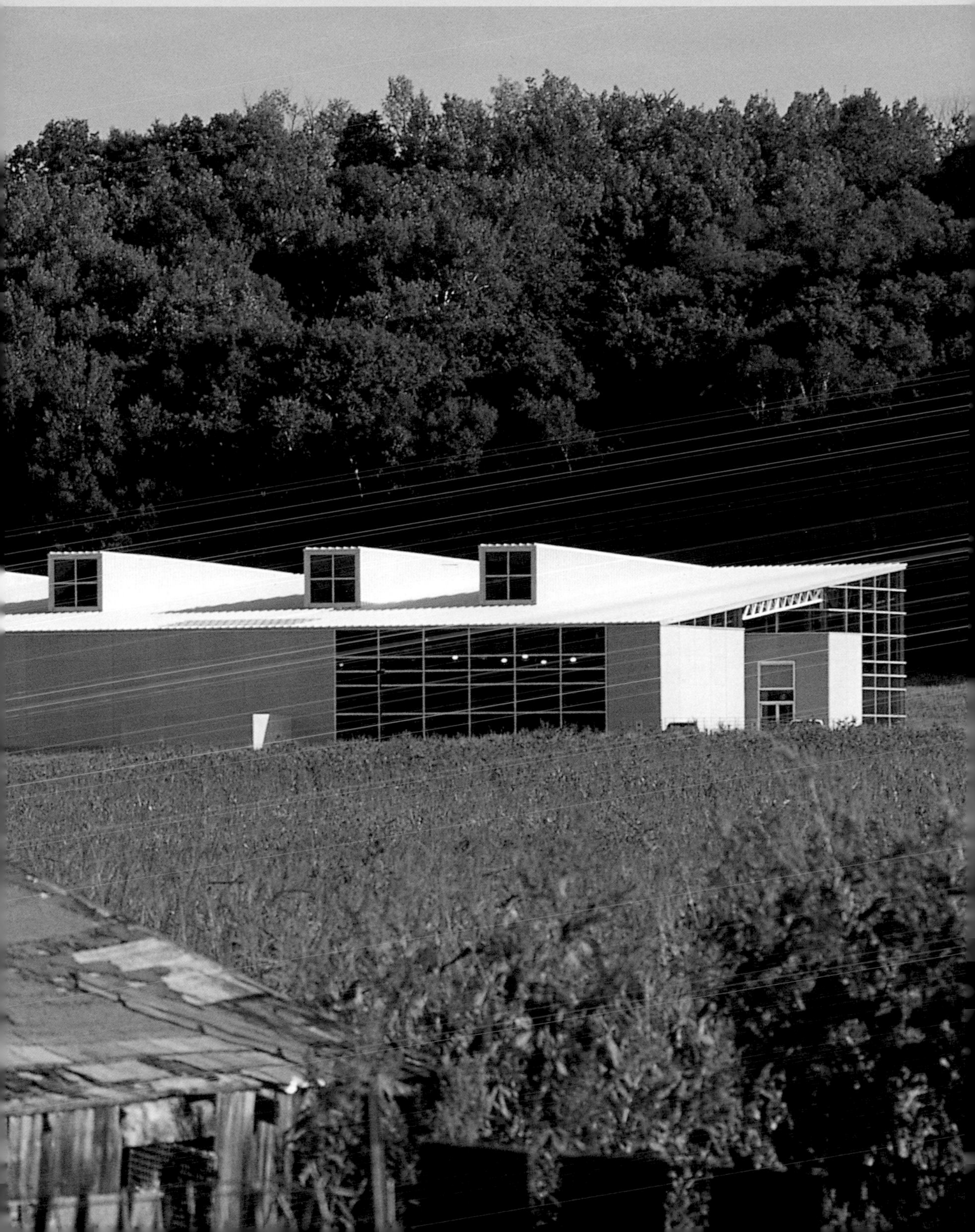

QMR Production   River Falls, Wisconsin   1996

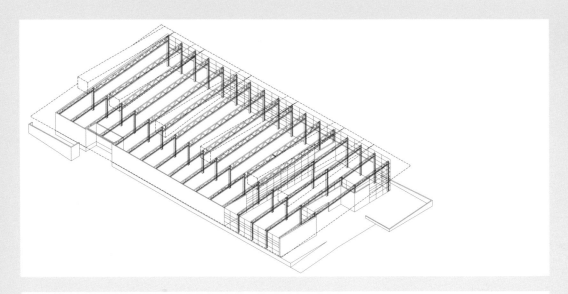

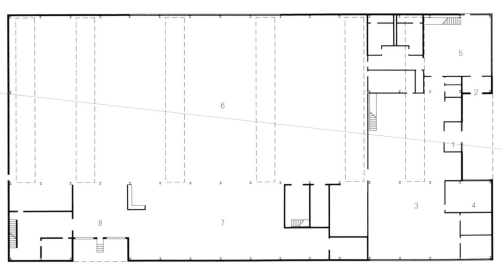

0   25   50

1. visitor entrance
2. employee entrance
3. open office
4. meeting room
5. lunchroom
6. press area
7. materials storage
8. shipping and receiving

The owner required a building that would attract and retain highly trained employees but never appear excessive or extravagant to clients. Simple forms and practical building assemblies combine with natural light and views to address the daily work experience of the staff. Accomodating three shifts per day, the building is continually occupied. The day is punctuated with views into the rural landscape and changes in light and weather. The site is a former agricultural field surrounded by a forested ridge.

We conceived the building as a simple, direct, and pragmatic structure. Entrances and the loading dock are cut into the building's simple shed form. Pre-engineered, manufactured trusses provide a ninety-foot span with twenty feet of unobstructed height, allowing a bridge crane to operate over the entire production floor. Water, electric, and compressed air are conveyed through tunnels below the floor. Precast-concrete tilt-slab panels and full-height glass enclose the factory.

Project Team
(James/Snow Architects)
Julie Snow
Vincent James
Grant Reiling
Krista Scheib
Doug Coffler
Nancy Blankfard
Craig Roberts
Nathan Knutson
Jim Larson

Structural Engineer: Meyer Borgman Johnson
Mechanical Engineer: Jack Snow
Electrical Engineer: Kaeding Associates
Landscape Architect: Shane Coen, Coen and Stumpf
Contractor: PCL Contractors
Photographer: Don Wong
Owner: Quadion Corporation

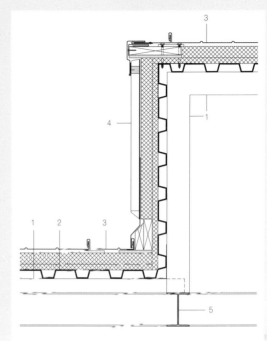

transverse section at roof articulation
1. steel tube
2. steel deck
3. raised-seam metal roof
4. raised-seam metal wall panel
5. steel-truss member

Product Engineering Minneapolis, Minnesota 1997

Product Engineering   Minneapolis, Minnesota   1997

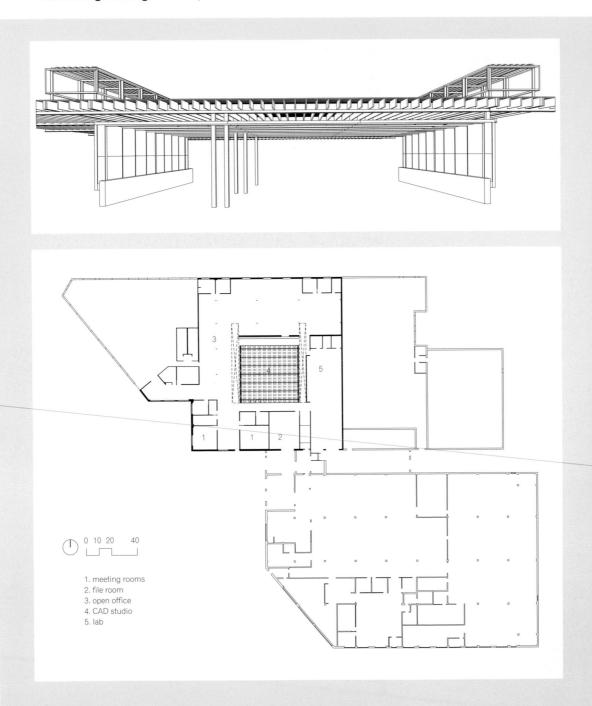

0 10 20   40

1. meeting rooms
2. file room
3. open office
4. CAD studio
5. lab

This project transformed fragmented, poorly lit offices into a unified collaborative workplace for product engineering. In the former spaces, CAD operators fixed cardboard shields around their monitors to reduce the glare of overhead lights. We began by removing ceilings, partitions, and portions of the roof to allow light into the center of the space. A central, suspended, light-diffusing hood defines the CAD group within the space and provides a controlled light environment for their work. The open ends of the hood allow collaboration with engineers. The frame assembly of steel plate, rods, and cotter pins permits the suspended polycarbonate panels to be dropped for cleaning and the lamping of fixtures. The presence of the frame in enclosed offices and conference rooms was minimized to increase transparency.

Project Team
Julie Snow
Christian Dean
Ben Awes
Jim Larson

Structural Engineer: Meyer Borgman Johnson
Mechanical Engineer: Jack Snow
Electrical Engineer: Kaeding Associates
Contractor: McGough Construction
Photographer: George Heinrich
Owner: Quadion Corporation

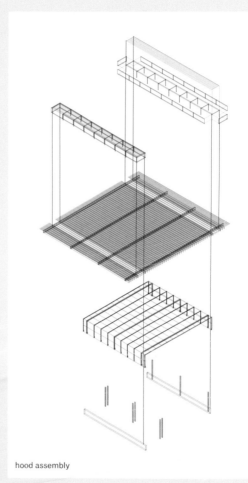

hood assembly

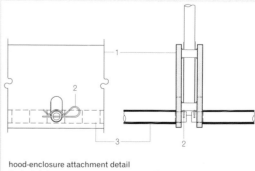

hood-enclosure attachment detail
1. steel plate
2. cotter pin
3. cellular polycarbonate sheet

Fifth Precinct Station Minneapolis, Minnesota 1999

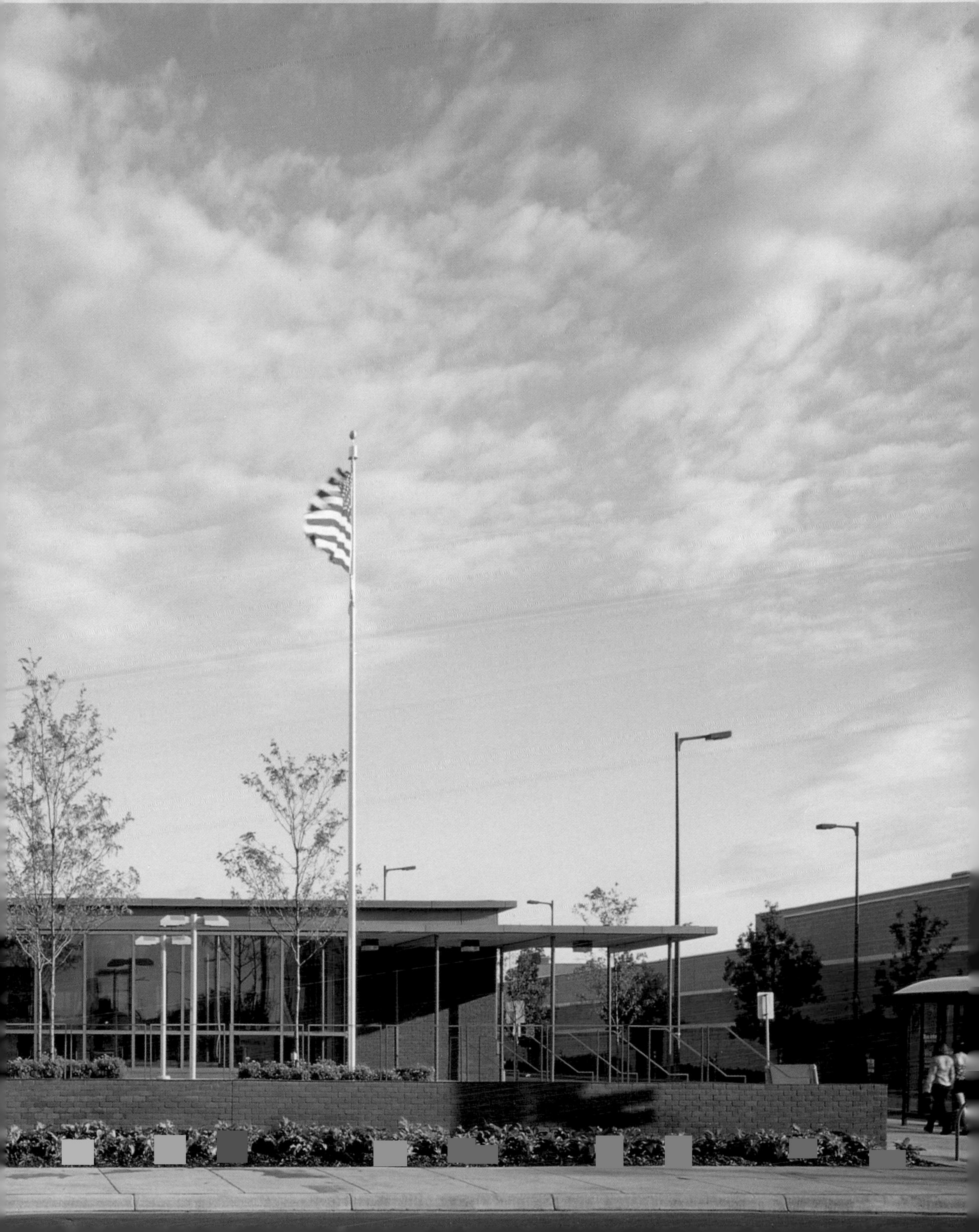

Fifth Precinct Station   Minneapolis, Minnesota   1999

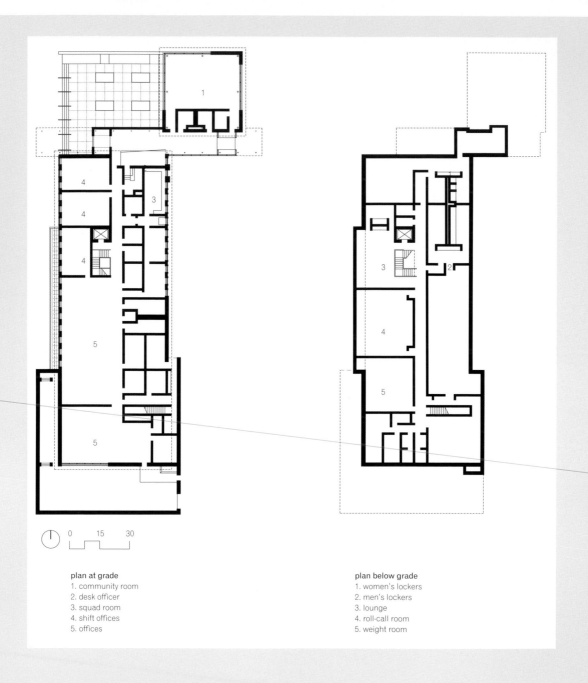

0   15   30

plan at grade
1. community room
2. desk officer
3. squad room
4. shift offices
5. offices

plan below grade
1. women's lockers
2. men's lockers
3. lounge
4. roll-call room
5. weight room

The City of Minneapolis invited architectural proposals for the first community-based police station. As the only firm with no previous precinct-design experience, we interviewed law-enforcement personnel and discovered how acutely aware they were of their building's vulnerability. Conversely, community-design participants were insistent in their desire for a "non-fortress-like" building.

Balancing these two opposing requirements, the project began with a simple, defensible volume housing police functions. Masonry and bullet-resistant glass with a stainless steel surround provide a protective enclosure. Another masonry wall wraps around the south end, creating an equipment court and a light well into the break room below as well as an additional protective layer. Perpendicular to this volume is a public zone comprised of a raised plaza, a community room, and a garden. An entry space joins the two volumes.

Project Team
Julie Snow
Krista Scheib
Ben Awes
Tom Van de Weghe
Mark Larson
Greg Larson
Todd Homber
Jim Larson

Structural Engineer: Mattson MacDonald
Mechanical Engineer: Jack Snow
Electrical Engineer: Kaeding Associates
Landscape Architects: Damon Farber Associates
Contractor: Sheehy Construction
Owner: City of Minneapolis

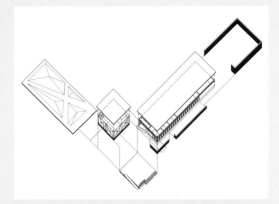

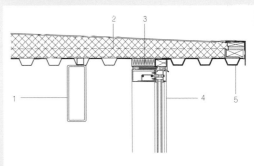

community room roof-edge detail
1. steel-tube beam
2. steel-tube outrigger
3. steel channel and insulation welded to outrigger
4. aluminium curtain wall
5. steel deck attached to spanning steel section

Jerstad Center The Good Samaritan Society Sioux Falls, South Dakota 1999

Jerstad Center The Good Samaritan Society Sioux Falls, South Dakota 1999

The Good Samaritan corporate offices are located on forty-seven acres of rolling prairie south of Sioux Falls, South Dakota. Under the leadership of Dr. Mark Jerstad, the client wished to develop partnerships to create new models of caregiving. The building was named in honor of Dr. Jerstad, who was diagnosed with cancer during the project and did not live to see its completion. The center's hybrid program consisted of overnight-stay rooms, meeting spaces, a video studio, an office space, and a dining area. A sense of retreat was to permeate the visitor's experience.

The creation of a sense of comfort and calm on the site was challenged by an interstate bordering the northwestern portion of the site and by a subdivision to the north. In addition, the Great Plains' hostile winds blow in from the northwest. Turning its back to the north and west, the building opens to the rolling acreage to the southeast. An outdoor terrace and pond take advantage of the microclimate created by the building's orientation. The long north leg of the building places the overnight-stay rooms along the water in a single corridor, far from the meeting rooms.

Precast walls protect the large public spaces. Clerestory glass-and-steel columns separate the walls from the timber roof. The glass walls are composed of three single-functioning layers: weather surface, wind brac-

ing, and structure. A thin section of aluminum glazing is stiffened laterally by a steel wind frame of double steel plates tied back to the steel columns. Zinc cladding and full-height windows, with internal wood shutters, enclose the overnight-stay rooms.

Project Team
Julie Snow
Doug Coffler
Ben Awes
Krista Scheib
Christian Dean
Mark Larson
Jim Larson
John Larson
Greg Larson
Todd Hemker
Mike Christiansen

Structural Engineer: Meyer Borgman Johnson
Mechanical/Electrical Engineer: Michaud, Cooley Erickson
Landscape Architect: Tom Oslund (with HGA)
Contractor: Sioux Falls Construction
Photographer: Richard Barnes
Owner: The Good Samaritan Society
Owners Representative: Steve Larson, NEXT, Inc.

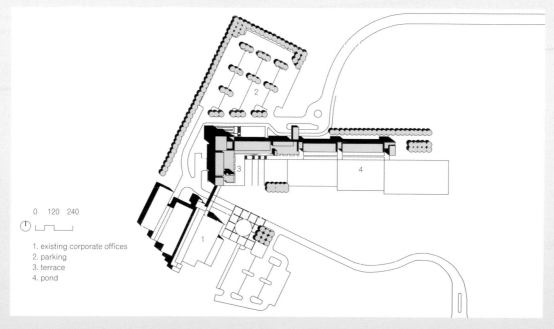

0 120 240

1. existing corporate offices
2. parking
3. terrace
4. pond

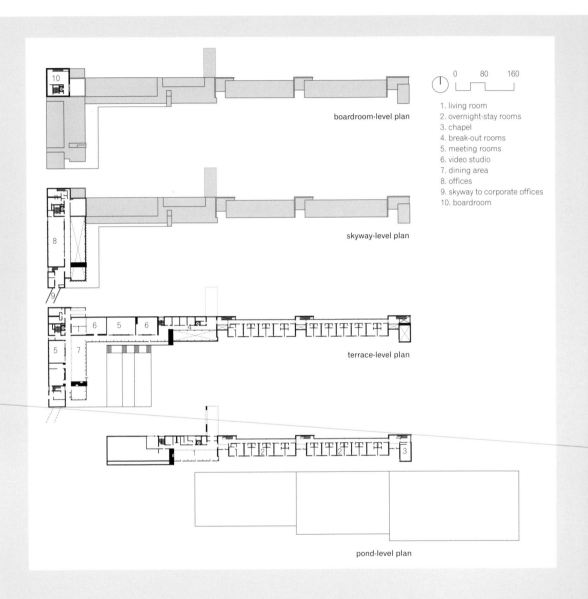

boardroom-level plan

0   80   160

1. living room
2. overnight-stay rooms
3. chapel
4. break-out rooms
5. meeting rooms
6. video studio
7. dining area
8. offices
9. skyway to corporate offices
10. boardroom

skyway-level plan

terrace-level plan

pond-level plan

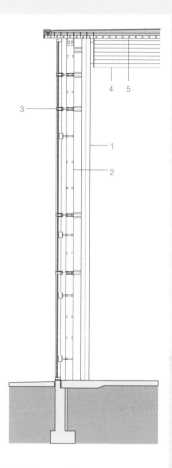

aluminum curtain-wall wind-frame section
1. steel column
2. steel wind frame
3. aluminum curtain wall
4. glulam beam
5. structural wood deck

Great Plains Software Fargo, North Dakota   2001

Extraordinary corporate growth required a design of eighty acres of plains south of Fargo, North Dakota, that retained a rich cultural connection to the landscape. Constructed elements were designed to operate like the most significant plains artifact: the planted shelterbelts. The site plan's east-west direction borrows from the plains' small towns, with main streets that terminate at the horizon, both to the east and to the west. All structures, buildings, plantings, and parking areas are linear forms that create shifting parallel planes that frame the horizon and create perspectival transformations when moving through the site.

The clients view their business as an ecosystem, adapting and responding to external forces as adeptly as healthy natural systems. Therefore, the building program developed in response to dynamic performance criteria rather than to fixed spaces. Integrated building systems create a mobile work environment, maximize bandwidth to the desk, offer direct user control as the most responsive system, and support both collaborative and individual work. Five distributed masonry-clad mechanical-equipment towers deliver low pressure, 65° air through a raised floor plenum. This warmer setting allows the use of outside air earlier in the fall and later into spring, reducing cooling loads and improving air quality. Air flow is controlled through user-operated floor louvers. Mobility is achieved through the ubiquitous data, phone, and power systems contained in the floor.

The architecture extends the site-plan strategy to intensify the experience of the plains landscape. Two volumes, one masonry and one glass, shift in relation to the other. The curtain wall and structural system are detailed to reinforce the sense of freely navigating through the plains. A visible two-inch gap resolves the connection between column and beam, actually realized within the raised floor plenum. The sill plate is placed below the floor surface, reinforcing a sense of lightness. High-performance glass reduces lighting loads and increases the visual clarity of the glass volume. We detailed the steel-and-glass volume for lightness, while the masonry volumes were designed to reinforce their solidity and mass. The masonry's dark tone gives it weight and contrasts the light sky and the seasonal color variations of the landscape.

Project Team
Julie Snow
Tom Van de Weghe
Christian Dean
Tim Bicknell
Connie Lindor
Bob Ganser
Craig Roberts
Nina Broadhurst
Ben Awes
Takuma Handa
Jim Larson
Lucas Alm
Tats Tanaka
Eric Tietz
Dan Clark
Rich Firkins

Landscape/Site Planners: Terry Harkness, Matt Torgerson
Structural, MEFP, IT, Acoustical Engineers: Leo Argiris, Chrystalla Kartambi, Brian Katz, Al Lyons, Nigel Tonks, Steve Walker, Arup
Lighting Consultant: Schuler and Shook
Food Service Consultant: Robert Rippe
Construction Manager: David Schultz
Photographer: Tim Hursley
Owner: Great Plains Software

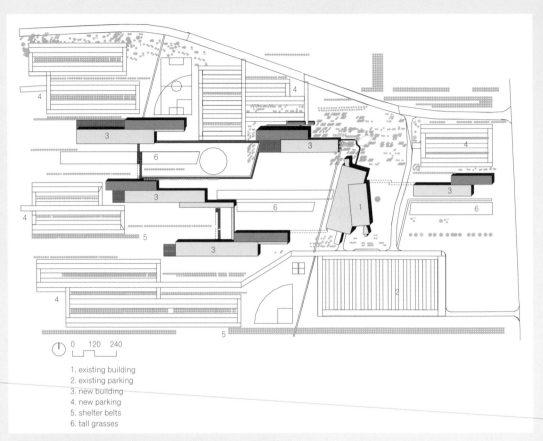

1. existing building
2. existing parking
3. new building
4. new parking
5. shelter belts
6. tall grasses

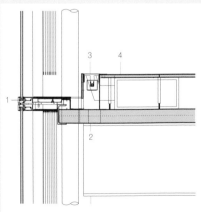

access-floor edge detail
1. aluminum curtain wall
2. composite steel deck
3. fin-tube radiation
4. raised access floor

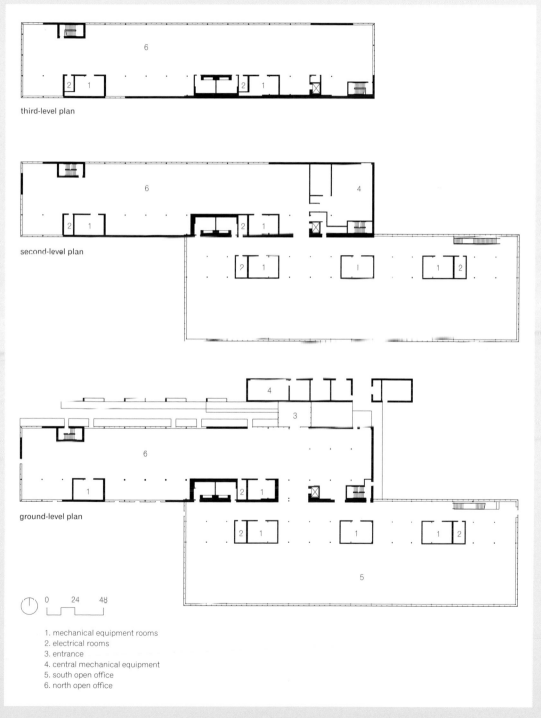

third-level plan

second-level plan

ground-level plan

0   24   48

1. mechanical equipment rooms
2. electrical rooms
3. entrance
4. central mechanical equipment
5. south open office
6. north open office

81

Koehler House New Brunswick, Canada 2001

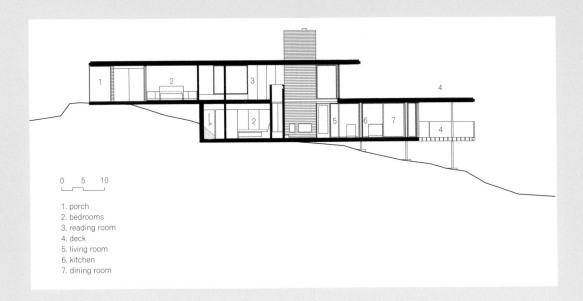

0 5 10

1. porch
2. bedrooms
3. reading room
4. deck
5. living room
6. kitchen
7. dining room

We visited this rugged, remote, stunningly beautiful site on New Brunswick's Bay of Fundy with the client in the early spring and immediately identified a rocky finger of land sloping east and south toward the bay as the building site. With the wind blowing from the west, the rocky slope protected us as we discussed the house, and standing on the ridge above permitted extraordinary views. Exposed granite, partially covered with a thin but dense mat of plant material, faces an uninterrupted ocean horizon.

A small building in a large landscape, the house affords expansive views but offers protection from the occasionally harsh climate. Two bars of living space cantilever from the rocky site, anchored by a stone wall. The thinnest possible membrane separates the interior from the majestic, sometimes threatening seascape. The floor, roof, and large sliding glass panels are detailed with a minimal section. Designed to resist the caustic marine environment, the exterior envelope is composed of glass, stone, stainless steel, and wood. In high winds, stiffened floor plates resist lateral loads. The structural design minimizes disturbance of the site.

Designed to remove the owners from their hectic schedules, the house intentionally slows the rituals of everyday life, allowing the presence of landscape to permeate every activity. We did not design for efficiency, but for various ways of connecting activity to place.

Two low, parallel cabinets contain the minimum equipment required for preparing simple meals while allowing unimpeded exposure to the vast landscape. The enclosed stair rises to frame an expanse of the ocean horizon. Both subtle and sudden changes in light, wind, and water modify every experience within the house.

Project Team
Julie Snow
Ben Awes
Connie Lindor
Lucas Alm
Kenwood McQuade
Jim Larson

Structural Engineer: John Johnson, Consultant; Cambell Comeau Engineering LTD
Mechanical Reviewer: Jack Snow
Geotechnical Engineer: Jacques Whitford
Contractor: ERB Builders
Photographer: Brian Vanden Brink, Steve Dunwell
Owner: Mary Beth and David Koehler

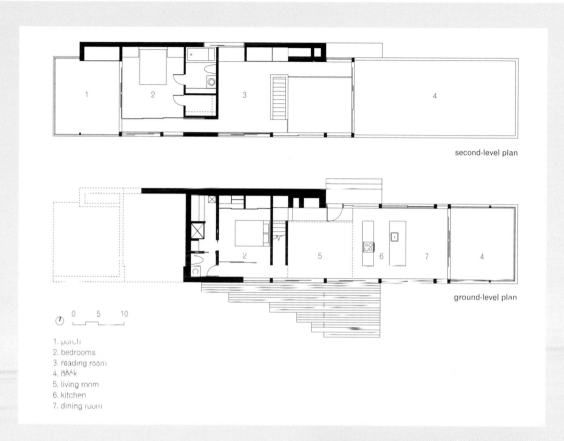

second-level plan

ground-level plan

0 5 10

1. porch
2. bedrooms
3. reading room
4. deck
5. living room
6. kitchen
7. dining room

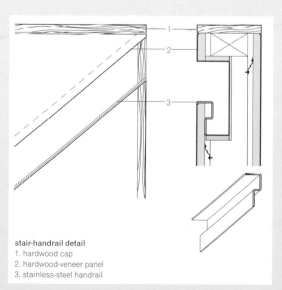

stair-handrail detail
1. hardwood cap
2. hardwood-veneer panel
3. stainless-steel handrail

Lake Street station section

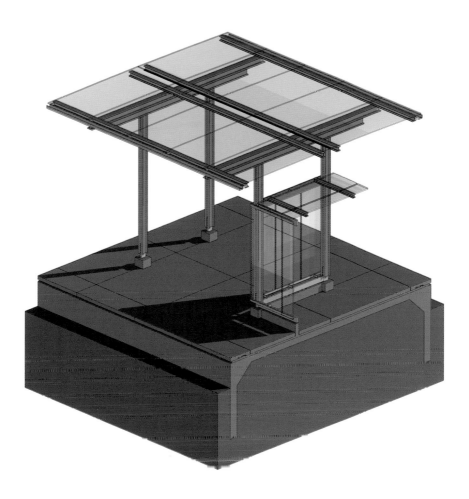

Cedar-Riverside station section

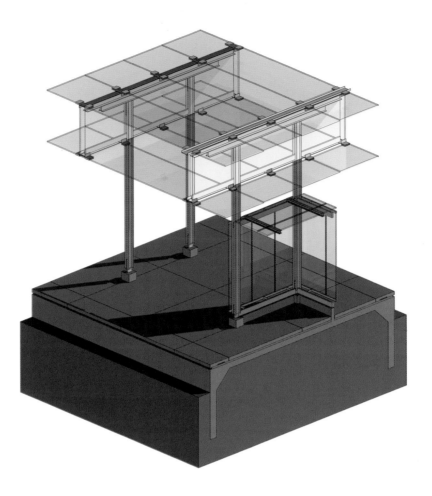

Nicollet Mall station section

Light Rail Transit Stations Minneapolis, Minnesota 2002

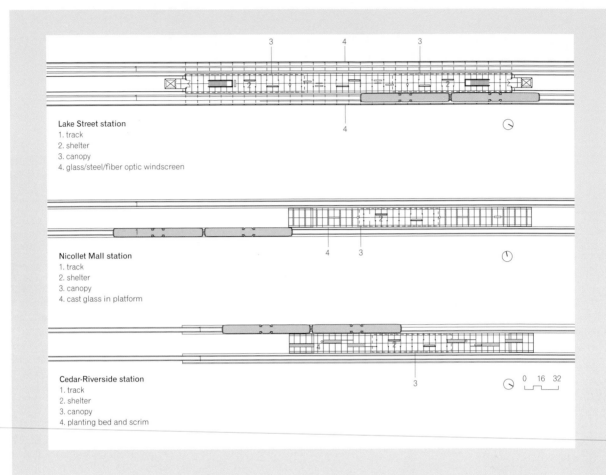

Lake Street station
1. track
2. shelter
3. canopy
4. glass/steel/fiber optic windscreen

Nicollet Mall station
1. track
2. shelter
3. canopy
4. cast glass in platform

Cedar-Riverside station
1. track
2. shelter
3. canopy
4. planting bed and scrim

0 16 32

Julie Snow Architects was selected to design three of thirteen light-rail transit stations for the city of Minneapolis. Each station responds to neighborhood qualities using a common structural system—glass, light, and movement. A simple post-and-beam structure insets the columns and forms an interior waiting area and passenger-loading platforms on each edge. To reduce the section of the beam, a double beam is used. The slightly shorter height of the lower beam strengthens the cantilever.

The Lake Street station is located in a car-dominated, low-rise commercial district. To create a landmark, we amplified the raised station's presence by extending the structure over the tracks on both sides. The sides carry linear bands of fiber-optic-lit steel and glass windscreens, which provide user comfort on the platform. Elevator towers house portraits, imbedded in laminated glass, created by a local photographer.

The Cedar-Riverside station is tucked behind residential high-rise buildings in a hidden corner of the city. The tall neighboring buildings provide passive surveillance through the glass canopy of this simple station. The approach to the station is marked with light green screens used for community gardens or as a canvas for artists' works.

The Nicollet Mall station, just off a major downtown Minneapolis shopping area, uses changing light and color to animate the street. Vertical panels of translucent glass are installed on each side of the paired steel-canopy columns, with fiber-optic tubing and small speakers inserted between the glass for changing orchestration of light and sound. Clear glass, above and below the vertical panels, forms a canopy over the waiting area. Set into the platform are illuminated cast-glass bands spaced at intervals similar to the canopy's glass panels.

Project Team
Julie Snow
Kenwood McQuade
Bob Ganser
Tim Bicknell
Lucas Alm
Tats Tanaka

Artist Collaborator: Tom Rose
Landscape Architect: BRW
Owner: Hiawatha Project Office, Minnesota Department of Transportation, Metropolitan Council

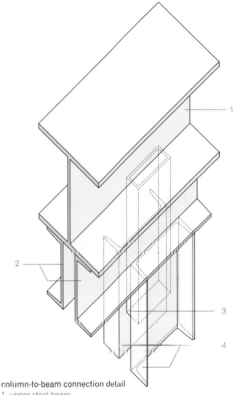

column-to-beam connection detail
1. upper steel beam
2. lower double-steel channel beams
3. vertical interior steel-cube section
4. double steel-channel column

School of Business University of South Dakota Vermillion, South Dakota 2001

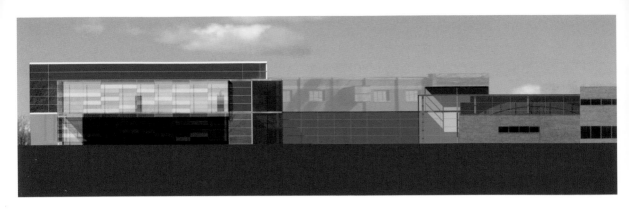

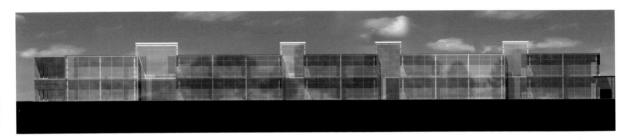

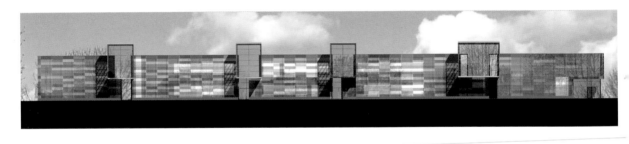

School of Business University of South Dakota Vermillion, South Dakota 2001

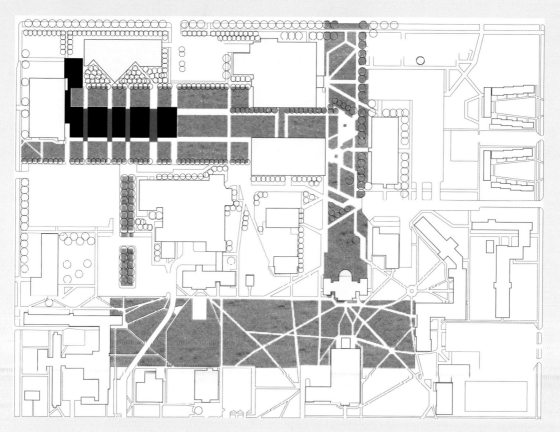

The University of South Dakota invited four firms to design a new School of Business. Its curriculum relied on the student's internet use for current business research. The project brief also included a commitment to demonstrating environmentally sustainable concepts. The campus contained several well-developed quadrangles; the competition site was a less-defined greenspace at the northwestern corner, used as a primary pedestrian entry to the campus.

As with most campuses in cold climates, students prefer to walk through building corridors rather than outdoors during the winter. We proposed an interior quadrangle formed by new buildings with circulation corridors replacing sidewalks and the traditional lawn supplanted by programmatic volumes. Between these volumes are active, social, media-rich seams, stitching together the business school spaces. Stairs, bridges, study spaces, and media displays activate the seams. The school's many public centers can be accessed through these interstitial spaces from parking areas

to the south. A major student circulation artery to the north links the school to the media and law departments. Only seminar rooms, which empty out onto break areas outside the flow of traffic, are located off this corridor. A media lab at the east end of the buildings faces the library and cantilevers over an outdoor space.

The wall section was designed as a "light jacket" on the building—creating a shimmery, indefinite presence evocative of the school's internet-based activity. The exterior wall with insulation and weather membranes is covered with a wood skin. Single glass panels at varied vertical angles reflect the richness of the prairie's dynamic skyscape. Top and bottom louvers open to ventilate the wall space in the summer. The seams provide stack-assisted ventilation, creating further energy savings by using more outside air.

Project Team
Julie Snow
Christian Dean
Ben Awes
Bob Ganser
Craig Roberts
Connie Lindor
Lucas Alm
Tats Tanaka
Chase DeForest

Structural, Mechanical, and Integrated-Technologies
Engineer: Arup
Landscape Architect: Tom Oslund, Oslund & Associates
Owner: University of South Dakota

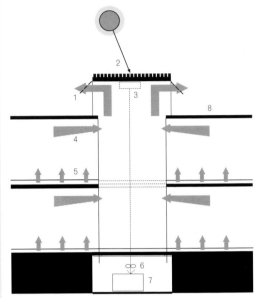

section diagram
1. motorized panels for midseason ventilation
2. photovoltaic panels—supplemental power to return-air fans
3. return air
4. cross ventilation generated by stack-assisted effect in seam
5. supply air
6. return-air fan
7. distributed-air handler
8. exposed concrete structure provides thermal mass

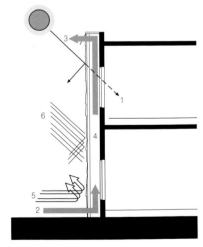

section diagram
1. solar reflection and summer solar-gain reduction
2. summer air infiltration
3. summer ventilation/winter heat retention
4. winter insulating cavity
5. wind-pressure reduction
6. rainscreen

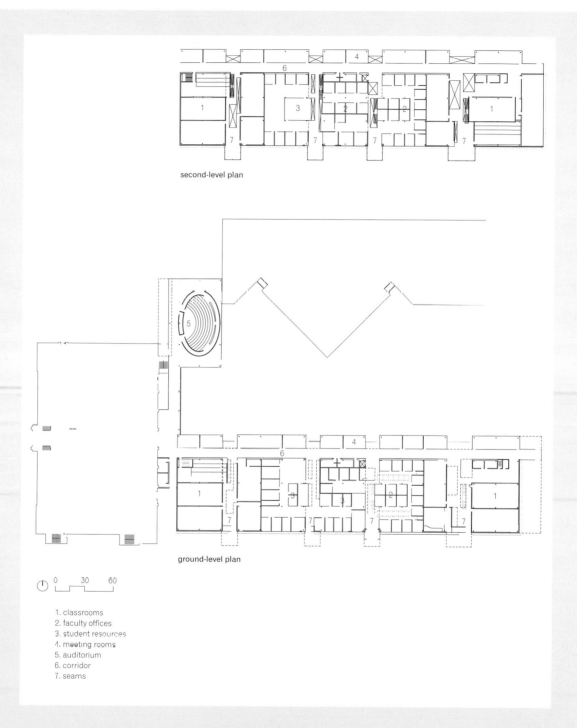

second-level plan

ground-level plan

0   30   60

1. classrooms
2. faculty offices
3. student resources
4. meeting rooms
5. auditorium
6. corridor
7. seams

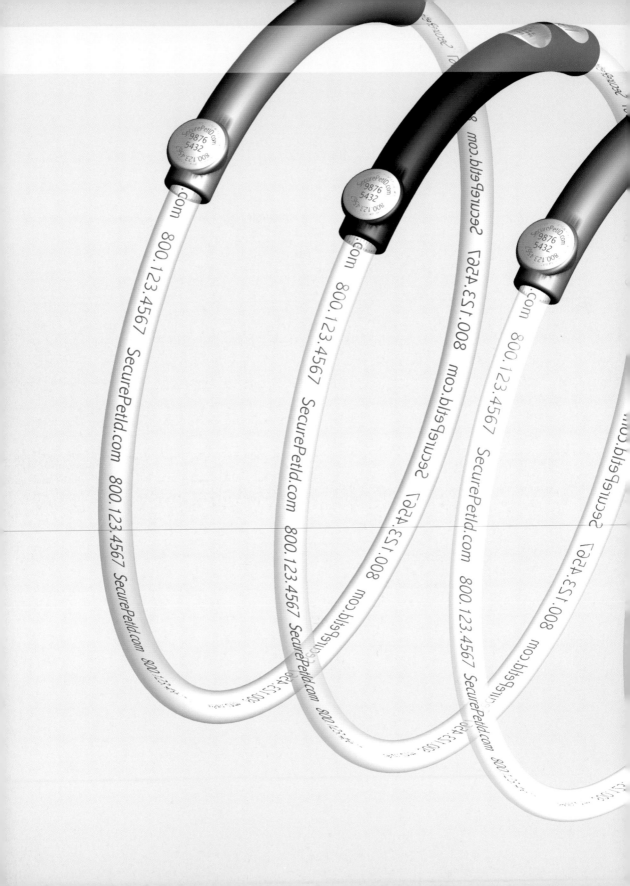

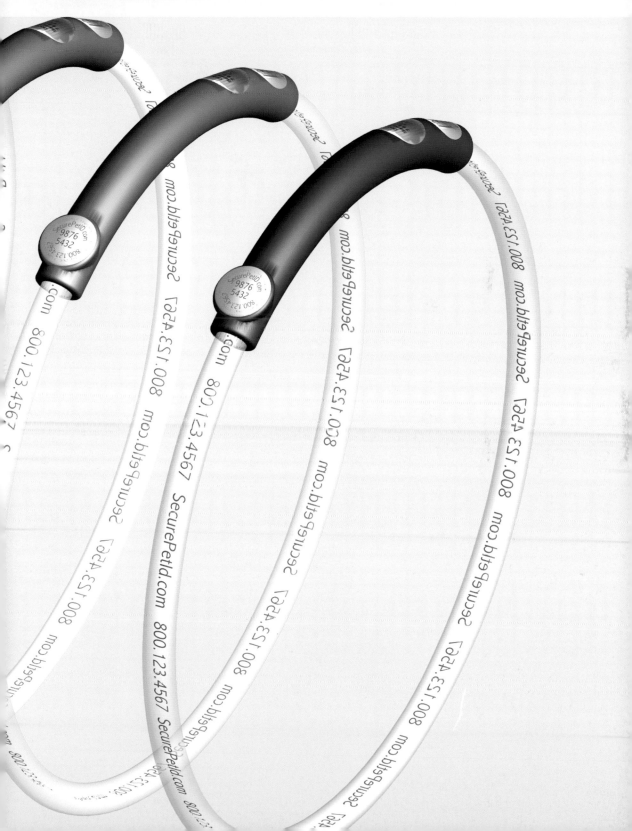

1. license tag
2. rabies tag
3. locking mechanism
4. flexible clear tubing with imbedded text

4 3 2 1

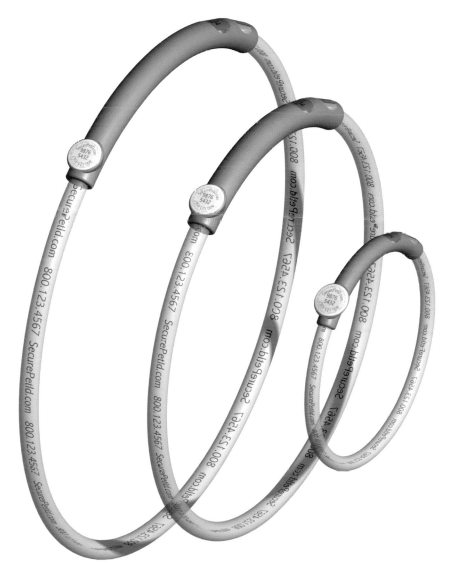

SecurePet ID Collar 2001

The SecurePet ID Collar uses radio-frequency identification (RFID) technology and a web-accessed database to return lost pets to their owners.

While it is easily identified as a pet collar, the SecurePet ID distinguishes itself from conventional containment collars. It is manufactured of translucent pliable plastic with printed information imbedded in an inner layer between two half-round translucent tubes, which are joined by the locking mechanism made up of a three-part, metallic, injection-molded plastic with an imbedded RFID chip. The collar locks onto the pet using a specially provided tool. Adhesive rabies vaccination and license labels replace conventional metal tags, making the collar quieter. Beads with individual letters and color disks allow owners to customize the collar based on pet name, personality, or season.

The locking mechanism contains a unique RFID tag and displays an identification number linked to the owner's data. A website and connected database facilitates the reunion of pets and owners. Additionally, a veterinarian collaborated with the design team to use the database to track and research animal diseases.

Project Team
Julie Snow
Connie Lindor
Lucas Alm

Manufacturing Engineer: Stan Buisman, QMR Plastics
Veterinary Consultant: Dr. Liz Lund, DVM
Web Designer: Tom Mayer, BSL Investments
Owner: Barrs Lewis, Principal; John Shorrock, Project
Manager; BSL Investments

Midtown Greenway Bridges Minneapolis, Minnesota 2002

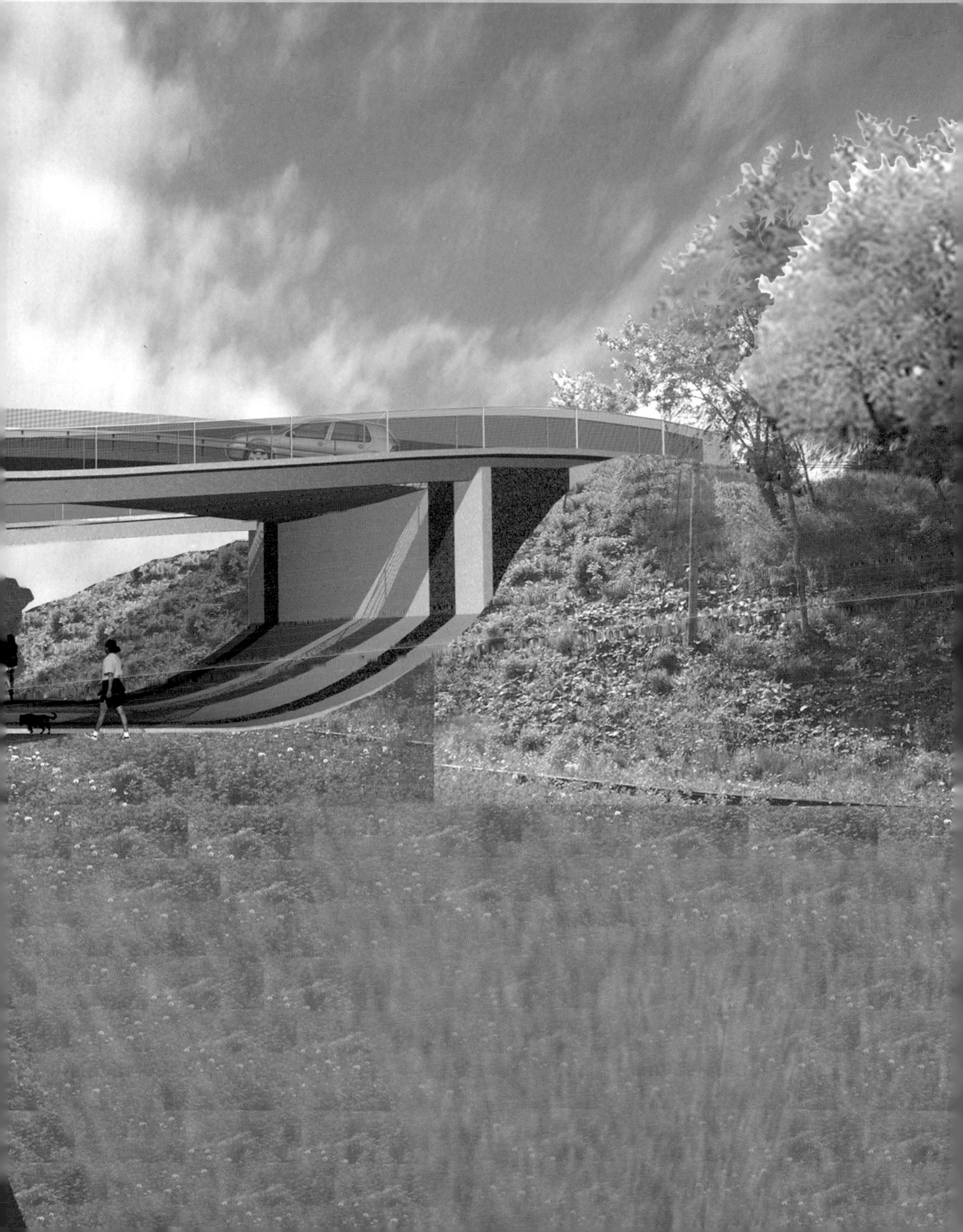

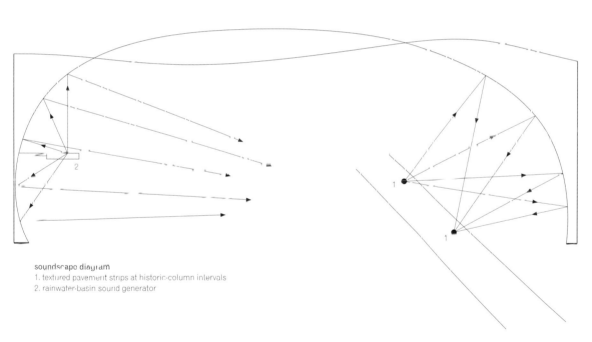

soundscape diagram
1. textured pavement strips at historic-column intervals
2. rainwater-basin sound generator

Midtown Greenway Bridges   Minneapolis, Minnesota   2002

During the early part of the last century, the need to separate train and car traffic resulted in a rail trench through Minneapolis. Today, the former railway is being transformed into a pedestrian and bicycle pathway, with a potential for future development of light-rail transit service. A design competition was initiated by the city to reconceive and replace the aging bridges that span the now defunct trench.

We approached the new bridges in a similar straightforward, utilitarian manner as the original designers. We separated the two pedestrian bridges from the vehicular bridge, letting them undulate and dip slightly below the road deck as they cross the greenway. In contrast, vehicular traffic rises gently to accentuate travel over the greenway and provides drivers with a glimpse of the space below. Pedestrians access the greenway by stairs at the Park Avenue bridge and by a ramp at the Chicago Avenue bridge. The resulting design inverts the past, connecting the life of the city above with the proposed greenway below, visually and kinesthetically.

Sound and light enhance the connection between spaces above and below the bridges. Parabolic abutments below the Chicago Avenue bridge create a playful, interactive soundscape. Fluted sound tubes cast into the bridge's concrete transfer sound from the greenway to Park Avenue at street level. Under the bridges, strips of textured pavement placed at the same intervals as the historic columns create sound as bicycles speed over them; a basin amplifies the

sound of falling drops of rainwater. Lighting on the bridges emphasizes movement. Recessed and hidden light sources illuminate the upper and lower surfaces of the bridge, while a continuous thread of light traces its undulating curve. A gentle, warm glow below the bridge underscores its structural lightness and the simplicity of the ribbon structure, its physical mass seemingly held aloft by light.

Project Team
Julie Snow
Martha McQuade
Ernesto Ruiz García
Zoe Adler Resnik

Artist Collaborators: Robin Minard, Matt Reinhert, Andrew Blauvelt
Structural Engineer: Leo Argiris, Arup
Landscape Architect: Bruce Jacobson, Close Landscape Architecture
Community Liason: Phill Lindsay
Owner: City of Minneapolis

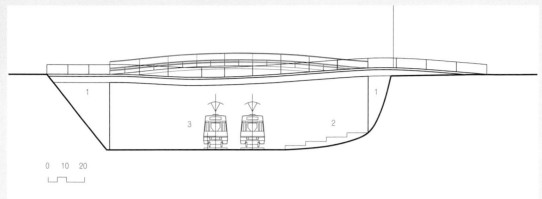

0 10 20

south elevation
1. vertical green wall connected to slope and rain garden below
2. terraced seating
3. future light-rail transit

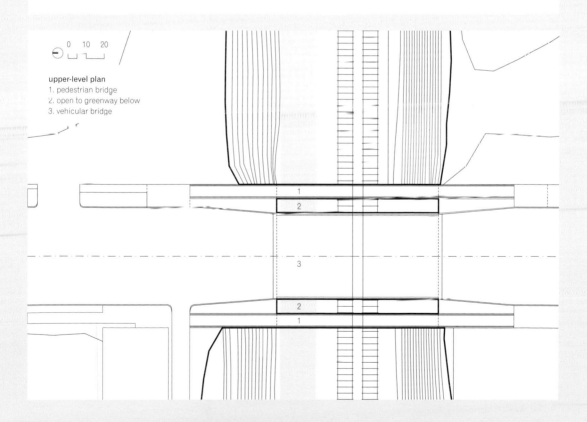

0 10 20

upper-level plan
1. pedestrian bridge
2. open to greenway below
3. vehicular bridge

Telematic Table Walker Art Center Minneapolis, Minnesota 2003

SELF PORTRAIT
CHUCK CLOSE

bracelet transponder, telematic table, and video projection
1. RFID tag on artwork wall label
2. passing the bracelet in front of tag encodes artwork ID
3. gallery visitors capture IDs, creating a personal collection of artworks
4. sensor in table reads each visitor's bracelet and displays collected artworks
5. video projection in lounge areas also displays collected artworks

4

5

information lounge video display

1. sensors read the visitors' transponder
   bracelets and display information on wall
2. computer analyzes collected data for
   possible connections
3. display shows connections among visitors

telematic table interactive displays
1. welcome and instructions greet users
2. table displays each user's collection
   and shows connections between artworks
3. table displays new shared content between
   artworks

1

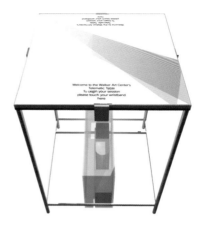

2

3

Telematic Table   **Walker Art Center**   Minneapolis, Minnesota   2003

The Walker Art Center invited five competition finalists to design an interface that fosters social interaction and information exchange in their new building. Our proposal assigns a unique digital aura to each visitor as a strategy to catalyze social interaction. The aura is personalized with information collected on a bracelet transponder that stores a mutable list of artworks and user preferences. Waving the bracelet near the art identifier, a wall-mounted transmitter placed beside each piece of art, adds that work to the visitor's collection. The art identifier writes the artwork's unique art ID on the bracelet. A second transponder at the Telematic Table reads the bracelet's information as the visitor approaches and instantly displays their collection in virtual galleries. The table interface graphically identifies similarities and differences among user collections to create conversational opportunities. For example, as visitors enter a lounge or café, their aura can be transmitted to a projector creating a gallery of visitor preferences. Returning visitors might continue to collect and access their collections at home through a reader transponder device, available at the museum shop.

The bracelet is a radio-frequency-identification (RFID) chip and transponder cast in tinted, translucent resin. The Telematic Table consists of a lightweight steel frame and a translucent surface. A cast-translucent box at its base holds a CPU connected to the Walker Art Center database and a digital projector. The table's surface is composed of three layers: a multi-user touch-screen mounted on an acrylic substrate with an amplification film that captures and enhances the digital projection. Bracelet sensors are concealed behind vertical stainless-steel cover plates at the edge of the table.

Project Team
Julie Snow
Dan Vercruysse
Takuma Handa

Software Designers: David Karam and Gigi Obrecht,
Post Tool Design
Multiuser Touchscreen Developer: Daniell Hebert, MOTO
Development Group

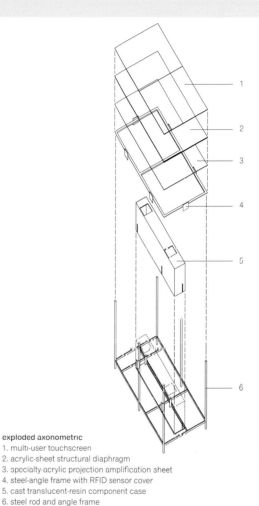

exploded axonometric
1. multi-user touchscreen
2. acrylic-sheet structural diaphragm
3. specialty-acrylic projection amplification sheet
4. steel-angle frame with RFID sensor cover
5. cast translucent-resin component case
6. steel rod and angle frame

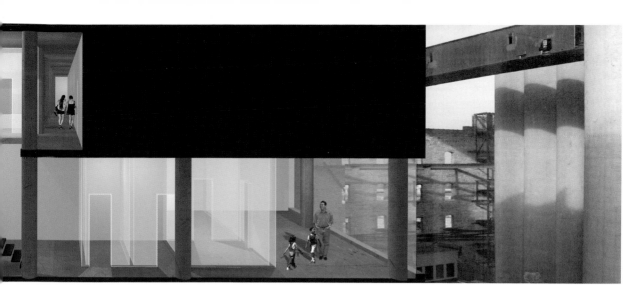

Humboldt Mill   Minneapolis, Minnesota   2004

The site for these condominiums is in the former milling district along the Mississippi River. The project proposed the renovation of an 1870s mill and new construction on an adjacent open lot. It is bounded by a former rail corridor to the south, planned for residential housing, and a 140-foot-tall grain elevator to the north. Historic-district guidelines limit the building height, require a masonry exterior with vertically proportioned "punched openings" (glass surrounded by masonry), and discourage projecting balconies.

The buildings contain three levels of parking with retail and housing lining the parking garage at street level and on the second floor. Upper levels and elevator lobbies are set back, separating the building's volume from the "historic" mass of the block and deferring to the height of neighboring structures. The lower floor layouts were challenged by the proximity and the shadows of a grain elevator located on the adjacent Mill City Museum and Ruins Park. The interlocking of two-story units offers city views and south light from the living areas and north light and views of the Mill City complex from the bedrooms. All units have exterior

access to terraces recessed in the south and east facades and to cantilevered balconies to the north.

The residences are designed to maximize the views of the city to the south with open floor plates of exposed post-tensioned concrete. Mechanical systems are similarly exposed in twelve-foot-high spaces. Light metal mesh railings create transparency, and floor-to-ceiling glass maximizes the presence of the city inside the residences.

The old mill is restored in compliance with historic guidelines, while the new annex modifies a strict composition of openings that respond to the placement of residences in the building. Corten-steel panels indicate the location of demising walls and the structural grid but, rather than duplicating them, shift one bay to the east to reveal concrete columns.

Project Team
Julie Snow
Ben Awes
Christian Dean
Bob Ganser
Tim Bicknell
Dan Vercruysse
Martha McQuade
Malini Srivastava
Ernesto Ruiz García
Zoe Adler Resnik
Kenwood McQuade
Craig Roberts
Jim Larson

Structural Engineer: Mattson Macdonald Engineers
Mechanical Engineer: Doody Mechanical
Electrical Engineer: Elliot Contracting Corp.
Civil Engineer: Hanson Thorpe Pellison Olson, Inc.
Acoustic Engineer: Arup
Contractor: Borson Construction
Photographer: Don Wong
Owner: Humboldt Lofts, LLC

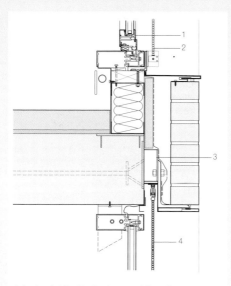

slab-edge detail with aluminum curtain wall
1. fixed stainless steel curtain
2. aluminum curtain wall with operable vent
3. steel-channel, brick-ledge angle connector
4. operable stainless steel curtain

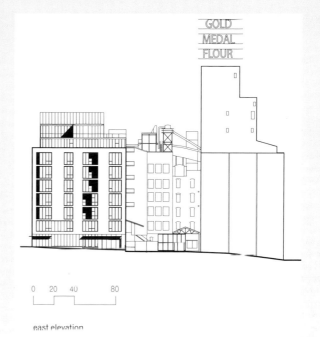

0   20   40   80

east elevation

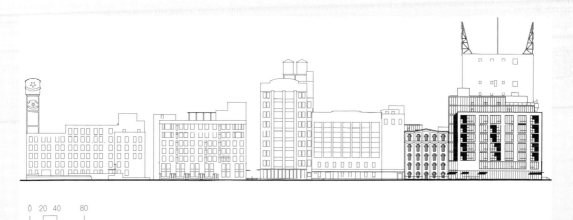

0 20 40   80

south elevation